What Keeps You in Your Seat?

by Mr. Grace's class
with Tony Stead

capstone

Introduction

by Margaret

What keeps you in your seat? It's *gravity*. Gravity is a force that is everywhere on Earth. It's even on other planets! Gravity is very important in our daily lives. Imagine trying to play a video game when the controller keeps floating away form you!

This book will educate you on forces, how gravity and mass relate, Sir Isaac Newton's three laws of motion, and how we use gravity in our everyday lives. You'll be on the edge of your seat while you learn about these important science concepts.

Forces

by Brooke, Evelyn, Jacqueline, Kaylinh, Laney

Have you ever pushed a shopping cart or fallen during a game of tug of war? If so, you have experienced a force. A force is a push or a pull. A push or a pull can be very simple. For example, a push could be pushing a person on a swing, and a pull could be pulling open a door. When you push or pull an object, the object moves in the direction of the force being applied.

Gravity is a major force in our lives. Gravity pulls objects toward each other. For instance when you throw a ball in the air, gravity pulls it toward Earth. Gravity is the force that pulls you down to Earth. In other words, it keeps you on the ground.

A push is an example of a force.

Machines can produce forces. Think about a crane. It lifts objects and puts them down. Now think of a bulldozer. It pushes objects out of the way.

Simple machines help us in everyday life by making work easier. Simple machines change the direction of a force and fight against gravity. A pulley is a simple machine. As you are trying to lift an object, gravity is pulling down on the object. However, the pulley will overcome gravity.

As you know, we constantly use forces in our lives. Objects such as construction equipment and shopping carts require forces to move and work. Forces help us accomplish many different tasks. So whenever you play tug of war or push a shopping cart, think of the forces you're using.

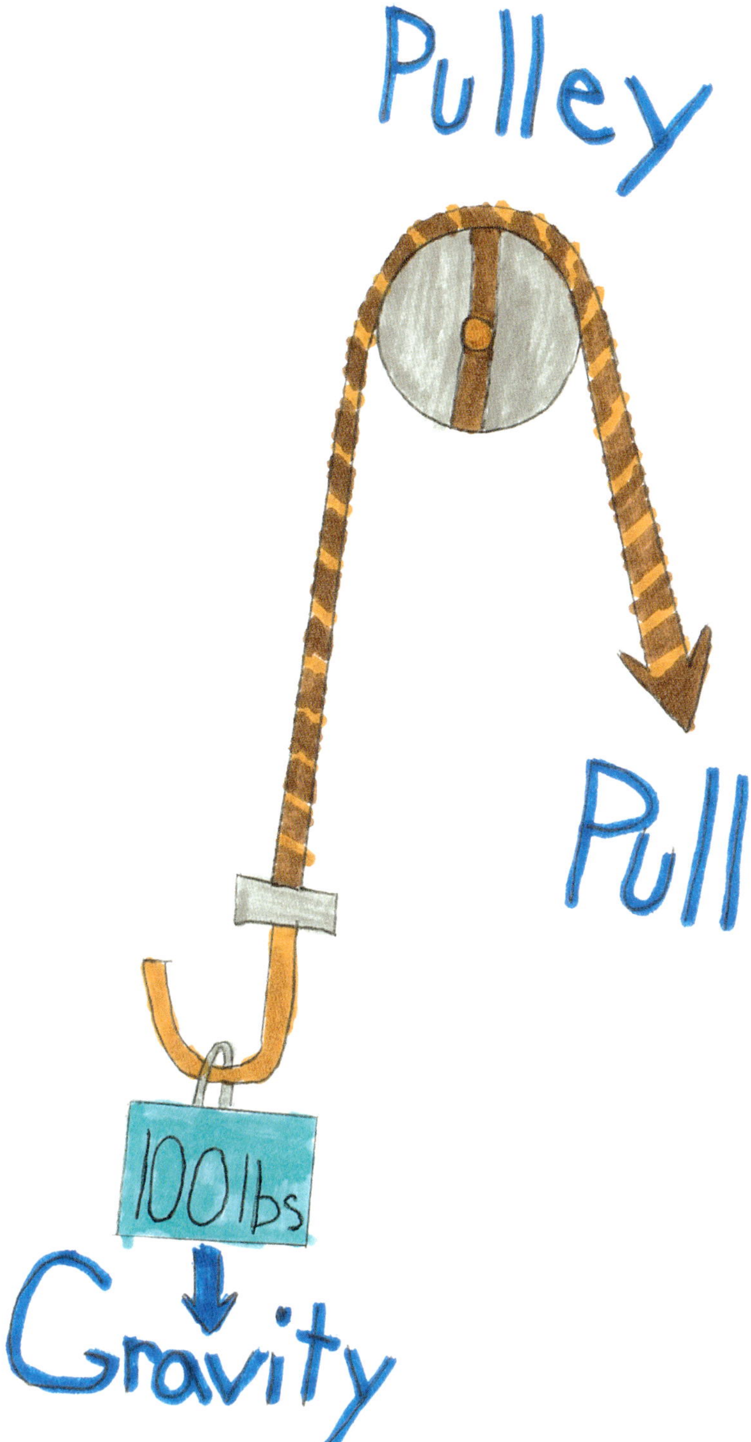
Pulley
Pull
100 lbs
Gravity

Mass and Gravity

by Bella, Ben, Brooke, Christian, Kaden, Makayla

You know what gravity is, but what is mass? How do they relate? We will explore how mass and weight are different and how mass relates to gravity.

Mass is the amount of matter in an object. The mass of an object not only depends on its size, but also on its composition, or the materials that make up an object.

A lot of people may think mass and weight are the same thing. They're not. Weight is the amount of force needed to keep an object down. Another way to say it is weight is the measurement of how hard gravity is pulling on an object. However, mass is the amount of matter in something. The mass of an object cannot change, but the weight can change based on the amount of gravity.

Any object with mass has gravity. If an object's mass is small, we don't feel its gravity. Earth's mass is large. Its gravity pulls us to the ground.

When you jump in the air, gravity pulls you back down to Earth.

Mass and gravity relate because the greater the mass of the object, the greater the gravitational pull it has. A gravitational pull causes massive objects to pull smaller objects toward it.

We know the Earth revolves around the sun, and the moon revolves around the Earth. The Earth has a greater gravitational pull than the moon because it has a greater mass than the moon. That means there is just enough gravitational pull from Earth for the moon to be able to orbit Earth.

Too Little

If there was not enough gravitational pull from the Earth, the Moon could possibly float around in the universe.

Just Enough

When there is just enough gravitational pull, the Moon is able to orbit around Earth.

Too Much

If there was too much gravitational pull, the Moon could possibly crash into Earth.

Fun Fact!

To escape our planet's gravitational pull, an object must travel seven miles a second.

Now that's Fast!

Why does the Earth orbit the sun? The sun's gravitational pull keeps our planet orbiting around it. All the planets have a gravitational pull. For example, because the sun is by far the largest object in our solar system, it extends its gravitational force far out into our solar system. Depending on the size of the planet or star, the gravitational pull changes.

Gravity and mass relate in many ways. These two concepts are important in space and in our lives on Earth.

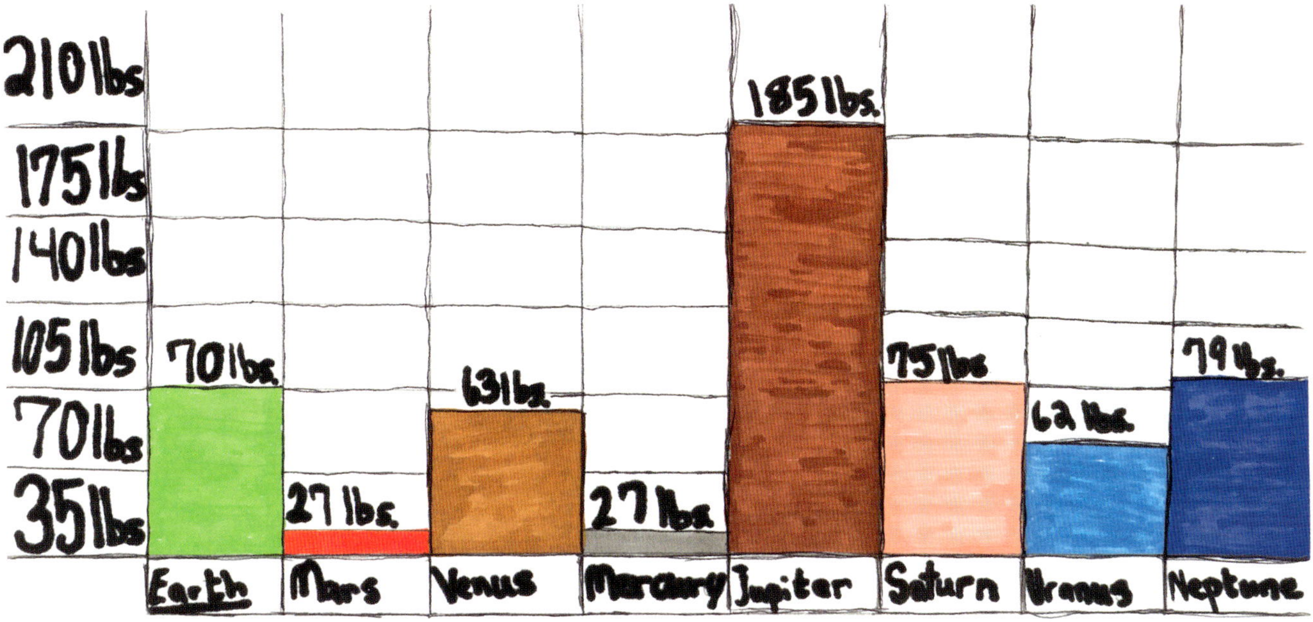

This graph shows how gravity would affect your weight on other planets.

Isaac Newton and the Laws of Motion

by Brooke, Connor, Julia, Julian, Kason, Lou, Matthew, Quannah, Seth, Walker

Sir Isaac Newton was a scientist who discovered the three laws of motion in the 1700s. We use these laws constantly in our everyday lives. In this chapter, you will learn how the laws connect to our lives and what life would be like without them.

Newton's first law states that an object in motion will stay in motion until an unbalanced force is applied. An object at rest will remain at rest until an unbalanced force is applied. This is also known as inertia.

Astronaut
Object at rest
Unbalanced force that is applied
Endeavour

Let's see how Newton's first law is used in our everyday lives. You're at a football game. Cam Newton throws the ball. Once it's in the air, gravity makes it come down. Let's say you are bowling. The pins are the objects that will remain at rest until a force is applied. The ball is the force being applied, making the pins fall down.

Imagine life without Newton's first law of motion. Let's say you're up to bat. The ball is pitched to you and you hit the baseball. Without the first law of motion, the ball would continue to fly forever! Because of gravity the ball comes back down to Earth. Newton's first law says the ball would stay in motion forever in a straight line at a constant speed until an unbalanced force is applied.

The force of the bowling ball causes the pins to fall down.

Newton's Second Law of Motion

When you kick a soccer ball, it goes pretty far. This is because of the second law of motion. An object will accelerate according to the amount of force applied to it and its mass. A heavier object requires more force to accelerate than a lighter object. For example, you'd have to kick a bowling ball with a lot of force to get it to go as far as a soccer ball. In addition to that, think about how much it would hurt your foot!

Have you ever wondered what life would be like without the second law of motion? Well, you wouldn't know a motorcycle can beat a truck in a race because the motorcycle is so much lighter. People wouldn't understand why empty shopping carts are easier to push than full ones. This is because of the relationship between mass, force, and acceleration.

Fun!

Ouch!

Newton's Third Law of Motion

Newton's third law is just as cool as his second law of motion. Have you ever gone bowling? When you throw or roll the ball, you stumble back. This is an example of Newton's third law of motion, which states with every action there is an equal and opposite reaction. The action is the ball going in one direction. The reaction is the ball pushing back on you, which causes you to stumble.

For example you're pushing on a wall. According to Newton's third law that is the action. This might sound strange, but the reaction is the wall pushing back on you!

Another example of Newton's third law is a bird flying and flapping its wings. The flapping of the wings is the action, which is the air pushing down from the wings. The reaction is the air pushing up on the bird. Remember that for every action, there is an equal and opposite reaction.

wings↓
(action)
↑air
(reaction)

Life would be much different without understanding Newton's third law of motion. If you were jumping, you'd fall through the floor because the floor wouldn't be pushing back on you. Newton's third law helps better understand why this doesn't happen.

Sir Isaac Newton was a scientist who helped us better understand how forces and motion affect our lives. So the next time you throw a touchdown pass like Cam Newton, think of Isaac Newton.

Sir Isaac Newton

Conclusion

by Margaret

Our lives would be completely different without gravity. Whether you're pushing a shopping cart or at the bowling alley, it affects the way we live our lives. So the next time you sit down in your seat, thank gravity for keeping you there. May the gravitational force be with you!